52
Checklist Essentials
My Small Business Notebook

Nina B

The 52 Week Experience Journal Series ©

All rights reserved. No parts of this book may be copied or reproduced for any reason in any form without written permission from the author.

First Print: Winter 2019

Ordering and Information contact

Opal Raye Publications

The52weekexperience@yahoo.com

443.567.8886

Baltimore, MD

There will always be someone rooting for you...

Thank you to all of those who continue to root for me.

Hey Future and Current CEOs!

52 essentials notebook is for:

- first timers in the business world,
- current business owners who need redirection to cover possible missed items in current business
- current business owners who want to add a new business and not wing it (like myself in the past)

If you find some task aren't needed for your industry or business, list N/A on the task and keep going. If you have more task than listed, add them to the bonus areas. Also use the notes areas for anything you need.

I am not an expert. I'm simply sharing some key items and tips I would have found helpful when starting in business myself.

Hopefully you will find this notebook to be a great roadmap in your journey.

Happy Building!

Nina B

Future CEO:

_____
_____
_____

What TYPE of business are you starting:

_____
_____
_____
_____

Reason(s) for starting this particular business:

_____
_____
_____
_____
_____
_____
_____
_____
_____
_____
_____
_____
_____
_____
_____
_____
_____
_____
_____
_____

NEVER FORGET WHY YOU STARTED

✓ Some things will have to give… List 10 things you are willing to sacrifice in your personal or social life for your business and success.

TIP: Put the listed items on post-its where you can see it daily to keep you focused

- ✓ Take a general Business class

    - ○ Location of class:
    _____
    _____

    - ○ Date Started and Completed:
    _____
    _____

    - ○ Key Items Learned:
    _____
    _____
    _____
    _____
    _____
    _____
    _____
    _____
    _____
    _____
    _____
    _____
    _____
    _____

    - ○ Cost (if any):
    _____

- ✓ Learn from those already in business. Intern or work in your industry/business at least 3 months.

    o Potential companies to work/intern:
    _____
    _____
    _____
    _____
    _____
    _____

TIP: Email companies noting intentions asking for internship and/or the opportunity to work with them. Have a trusted resource review your email prior to sending. Include brief bio and resume specific for industry.

    o Company selected:
    _____
    _____

    o Key Items Learned:
    _____
    _____
    _____
    _____
    _____
    _____
    _____
    _____
    _____
    _____

    o Date Started and Completed:
    _____
    _____

- ✓ City, State or Government Requirements.

Are there any required certifications, trainings or classes specifically needed for industry?

- Certifications, trainings or classes required:

_____
_____
_____
_____
_____
_____
_____
_____
_____

- Where/When to obtain requirements:

_____
_____
_____
_____
_____
_____

- Date(s) Completed:

_____
_____
_____

- Cost (if any):

_____

✓ The more you know... Before you jump in, take time to research your intended business/industry in the area(s) you intend to target. What are the demographics?

- Intended target area:

_____
_____
_____

- How many men/women/children and age ranges:

_____
_____
_____
_____

- How many in the same industry in the target area:

_____
_____
_____
_____

- How far apart are each of the same type of businesses:

_____
_____
_____
_____

- ✓ Target Market. Who will be helped by your service/product?
  - ○ Who are your intended clients:

_____
_____
_____
_____
_____
_____
_____
_____
_____
_____
_____
_____
_____
_____
_____

- ✓ Plan of action. Create a marketing plan to get your products/services into area or to clients listed above.

_____
_____
_____
_____
_____
_____
_____
_____
_____
_____
_____
_____
_____
_____
_____
_____
_____

✓ Business can be up and down. Are you prepared to keep running if you are in a slow season for business?

TIP: Save $500-$1000 for unexpected business cost.

- Slow season(s) in business:

_____
_____
_____
_____
_____
_____
_____
_____
_____
_____
_____

- Plan to boost business during the slow season:

_____
_____
_____
_____
_____
_____
_____
_____
_____
_____
_____
_____
_____
_____
_____
_____
_____
_____

✓ Save extra money for business and build better habits for business. You will need a jar or box with lid. Pay yourself weekly and/or daily by doing things to grow your business. Make a list of business habits you would like to create or business task you don't particularly like to do. Place a realistic dollar amount next to each task. Each day pay yourself for completing each task. At the end of your 30/60/90 days (you set the timeline. Minimum 30 days) tally up what you have saved and treat your business to something needed for growth. Cheating only cheats you and your business. Happy Building and Saving!

TIP: start with 3-6 task. You do this task as often as you like creating a new list.

- Date Started:

_____

- Positive habits to create (ex. Being on time, checking emails, reading more, etc.):

_____
_____
_____
_____
_____
_____
_____
_____

- Negative habits to break (ex. Not responding to clients in timely manner, not following up on business, etc.):

_____
_____
_____
_____
_____
_____
_____
_____

Save extra… Continued…

- How much will each task reward:

_____
_____
_____
_____
_____
_____
_____

- How long will you build this goal jar:

_____
_____
_____

- Date ended:

_____

- Total Reward Saved:

_____

- What was done with reward:

_____
_____
_____
_____
_____
_____
_____
_____
_____

✓ There's free money available for small businesses and entrepreneurs. Apply for business grants.

- Business Grants available:

___

- Documents needed to apply:

___

Grant... Continued...

- Business Grants applied for:

- Business Grants approved/grant gift:

- What was done with reward:

CHASING THE PASSION LAST. POPULARITY FADES. THE PAYCHECK WILL COME.

✓ It's all in the name. What is your Business/brand name going to become?

TIP: Select a name that will appeal to your target market, demographics and all potential client base.

- What is the name of your business and reason for choosing:

_____
_____
_____
_____
_____
_____
_____
_____
_____
_____
_____
_____

✓ Many times, entrepreneurs feel as if there are never enough hours in the day and many times there aren't (lol) however, creating realistic business hours and a schedule for emails, social media post and calls could remove the feeling of being overwhelmed.

TIP: Taking a time management class to help with prioritizing and time structure could help also.

TIP: USE YOUR CALENDAR AND ALARM CLOCK. When our packed schedules and our cluttered minds fail us- the calendar and alarm clocks are the best to keep appointments, events, task and more on the forefront. Log everything and have a back-up.

- o Business/Administrative/Meeting hours:

_____
_____
_____
_____
_____
_____
_____

- o Days/Hours for Emails and Calls:

_____
_____
_____
_____
_____
_____
_____

- o Days/Hours for Social Media Post/ Engagement:

_____
_____
_____
_____
_____

TIP: Use sites good for social media post planning.

✓ On IRS.gov Apply for EIN/tax ID. Can be listed under your legal name, brand or company name. Takes a few minutes and its Free.

TIP: If filing under brand or business name, complete visit to State building task before applying.

- EIN/Tax ID#:

_____
_____

✓ Visit your State building to Trademark business name and list business type with state.

What type of business are you? Sole Proprietor, Limited Liability Company, Partnership or Corporation.

TIP: If applying in person there may be a fee to expedite items However, it can be approved the same day. Mailing needed documents can take a few weeks for approval.

Sba.gov is a great site for defining each type of business.

- Type of business:

_____

- Required documents for approval (if any):

_____
_____
_____
_____

- Date approved (this is your official anniversary date):

_____

- Cost (if any):

_____

✓ If business will expand beyond your state- Trademark brand/business/logo nationally visit uspto.gov

- Required documents for approval (if any):

_____
_____
_____
_____
_____

- Date submitted and approved:

_____
_____

- Cost (if any):

_____

✓ Where are you running your business from?

Apply for a business license in the same county/city/state from where your business is based. To review business types and processes to apply, (from the web) type www.(yourstate).gov (ex. www.Maryland.gov) and go to the area for new business for licensing information.

Business base location:

_____
_____
_____

- Business license type:

_____
_____
_____

Business license… Continued…

- Required documents for approval (if any):

  _____
  _____
  _____
  _____
  _____
  _____
  _____

- Date approved:

  _____

- Cost (if any):

  _____

✓ Begin building business credit and open a business bank account.

  - Bank selected for account:

    _____
    _____

  - Required documents to open account (if any):

    _____
    _____
    _____
    _____
    _____
    _____

Bank acct... Continued...

- Requirements to maintain business account:

_____
_____
_____
_____
_____

- Perks of business account:

_____
_____
_____
_____
_____
_____
_____

✓ Stay Motivated and Encouraged but how? Create a plan to stay in the game.

TIP: following positive social media influencers in your industry, watching entrepreneur movies, finding daily quotes and more can help.

- ME (motivated and encouraged) Plan:

_____
_____
_____
_____
_____
_____
_____
_____
_____
_____
_____
_____

BE PATIENT WITH YOURSELF AND BUSINESS GROWTH

- ✓ Public listings. Grab your business name via domain/website and social media.

    - ○ Website name:

    _____

    - ○ Social Media handle(s):

    _____
    _____
    _____
    _____
    _____

    - ○ Cost (if any):

    _____

- ✓ What will your company stand by for its clients? Create Mission statement for business.

    - ○ Mission Statement:

    _____
    _____
    _____
    _____
    _____
    _____
    _____
    _____
    _____
    _____

- ✓ You are in an elevator on the top floor. There is another traveling to the lobby with you. During the trip down, you are asked what you do. You have 1-2 mins MAX to sell yourself and possible gain a new client. What is your elevator pitch?

- Elevator Pitch:

_____
_____
_____
_____
_____
_____
_____
_____
_____
_____
_____
_____
_____
_____
_____
_____
_____
_____
_____
_____
_____
_____
_____
_____
_____
_____
_____
_____
_____
_____

✓ What is your profit/loss margin? What's your company's value? How much will you owe the IRS? What are your business expenses (daily/monthly/yearly)? How much and how do you pay yourself?

Bookkeeping/taxes/financial planning will make a HUGE difference to you and your business.

TIP: Take a class and stay on top of tax laws/requirements for small business. Research and Hire a bookkeeper if needed.

- o Location of class:

_____
_____

- o Date Started and Completed:

_____
_____

- o Key Items Learned:

_____
_____
_____
_____
_____
_____
_____
_____
_____
_____
_____
_____
_____
_____

- o Cost (if any):

_____

✓ Create a Weekly/monthly profit/sales goal plan.

- How much will you need to make each day or week to cover business cost:

_____
_____
_____

- Plan to make and surpass daily/weekly goals for profit:

_____
_____
_____
_____
_____
_____
_____
_____
_____
_____
_____
_____
_____

✓ Ching Ching! How will you take payment from clients?

  - Accepted forms of payment:

_____
_____
_____
_____
_____
_____

✓ Are you covered? Look into business Insurance

  - Insurance Company:

_____
_____

- Coverage Type and amount:

_____
_____
_____

- Cost (if any):

_____

✓ One of the best pieces of business advice I was ever given was that "documentation beats conversation". Create contracts/terms and conditions for business.

TIP: Lock documents so no unapproved changes can be made but make documents fillable for receiver.

- Contract/Agreement types needed:

_____
_____
_____
_____
_____
_____
_____
_____
_____
_____
_____
_____
_____

✓ Starting and Running a business can be stressful. How will you destress?

TIP: Mentally and Physically care for yourself FIRST and you will be able to keep caring for business.

- o Destress Plan/Activities:

_____
_____
_____
_____
_____
_____
_____
_____
_____
_____
_____
_____
_____
_____
_____
_____
_____
_____
_____
_____
_____
_____
_____
_____

THE WORLD IS READY FOR YOU TO LEAVE YOUR MARK

- ✓ Photoshoot for Professional headshots, product and/or service

  - o Photographer and photoshoot location:

  _____
  _____

  - o Photo Package:

  _____
  _____

  - o Cost (if any):

  _____

- ✓ Leave your mark #1. Logo

TIP: Have one great logo that can transfer for and onto many items OR have a main logo for online and a secondary for products

  - o Color scheme:

  _____
  _____

  - o Logo idea/concept:

  _____
  _____
  _____
  _____

  - o Graphic Designer:

  _____

  - o Cost (if any):

  _____

- ✓ Leave your mark #2. Business cards and Flyers

TIP: KEEP THEM ON YOU AND LEAVE THEM EVERYWHERE!

- Information listed on business cards:

_____
_____
_____
_____
_____
_____
_____
_____
_____
_____
_____

- Information listed on flyers:

_____
_____
_____
_____
_____
_____
_____
_____
_____
_____
_____

- Graphic Designer:

_____

- Cost estimate:

_____

✓ Leave your mark #3. Branding and/or giveaway items specific for your business. Ex. Hair stylist may have bonnets, scarfs or combs or Chefs may have aprons or seasoning samples

   o Branding/Giveaway items:

   _____
   _____
   _____
   _____
   _____
   _____
   _____
   _____
   _____
   _____
   _____
   _____
   _____
   _____
   _____
   _____
   _____
   _____
   _____
   _____
   _____
   _____
   _____
   _____
   _____

   o Cost estimate:
   _____

- ✓ There's no place like home. Build a Website for everything for your company to funnel from.

TIP: Research hosting site for one that will work best for your needs, ease of use and cost.

- o Web hosting site:

_____
_____

- o Web designer:

_____
_____

- o Published Date:

_____
_____

- o Cost (if any):

_____

- ✓ Create social media marketing plan/calendar. Note traditional holidays and social media holidays.

  - o Social Media and Industry Specific Holidays:

_____
_____
_____
_____
_____
_____
_____
_____
_____
_____

- ✓ PSA! Send out mass messages to friends and family to inform them of your new business asking for their support and referrals.

    TIP: Be clear on the kind of support needed. Include electronic flyer, website and social media handles. Ask a trusted resource to proofread before sending out.

    - o Draft wording:

    _____
    _____
    _____
    _____
    _____
    _____
    _____
    _____
    _____
    _____
    _____

- ✓ Stock inventory and/or business supplies.

    - o What are the monthly necessities to operate business:

    _____
    _____
    _____
    _____
    _____
    _____
    _____
    _____
    _____
    _____
    _____
    _____

    - o Cost estimate:

    _____

- ✓ How to do what you do? Create Standard Operating Procedures.
    - ○ List of task that will need SOPs:

    _____
    _____
    _____
    _____
    _____
    _____
    _____
    _____
    _____
    _____
    _____
    _____
    _____
    _____
    _____
    _____

- ✓ Independent contractors and employees. Are you ready to build a team? If not ready to bring in others, still complete the next 3 check task as you are a still a one man or woman team.
    - ○ List state/city laws that apply to you having them:

    _____
    _____
    _____
    _____
    _____
    _____
    _____
    _____
    _____

- ✓ Everyone brings something to the table in business.

- What will you have to offer potential staff working with/ for your business:

___

- What are you looking for from staff working with/ for your business:

___

✓ Who does what in the company?

  - List job descriptions and duties

✓ Let everyone know you are here! Host Launch event or business warming. Use the opportunity to introduce your business publicly.

TIP: Have signup sheet for email/text list.

TIP: No funds for an event? Host online with a link for supporters to send gifts, book services and/or purchase products.

- o   Launch Date and Time:

_____

- o   Event Location:

_____
_____

- o   Event Goal:

_____
_____
_____
_____
_____
_____
_____
_____
_____
_____
_____
_____
_____
_____
_____
_____
_____
_____

Launch Party… Continued…

- o   Event Timeline:

_____
_____

_____
_____
_____
_____
_____
_____
_____
_____
_____
_____
_____
_____
_____
_____
_____

- Staff Count and Task:

_____
_____
_____
_____
_____
_____
_____
_____

- Cost (if any):

_____

BRING FOCUS NOT FEELINGS WHEN AT THE TABLE FOR BUSINESS

✓ Create a Vision board for your business. List photos and words that will motivate, empower and encourage you and that represent what you want in and for business over the next 1-3 years.

TIP: Hang board in a place you will see daily for the reminder.

- TOP 5 goals:

_____
_____
_____
_____
_____
_____
_____
_____

- Plan(s) to reach goals:

_____
_____
_____
_____
_____
_____
_____
_____
_____
_____
_____
_____
_____
_____
_____
_____
_____
_____
_____

✓ Knowing your Strengths are good but knowing your Weakness is equally important. Register for classes/seminars to improve upon your weakness.

TIP: Some things we struggle with can be the thing that can hold up business growth. If AFTER exhausting all resources- consider hiring someone.

- Weakness:

_____
_____
_____

- Class/Seminar:

_____
_____

- Location:

_____
_____

- Key Points Learned:

_____
_____
_____
_____
_____
_____
_____
_____
_____

- Cost (if any):

_____

✓ Connect with a Business Mentor and or business buddy. Doesn't have to be someone in same industry. Someone you can bounce items off of and/or one you can grow with in business.

- Business Mentor or Buddy:

_____

- How often will you meet:

_____
_____

✓ Set up information tables and/or vend at events/expos

TIP: Have signup sheet for email/text list, business cards, flyers and any giveaway items at each event.

- Potential Expos/Events to be a part of:

_____
_____
_____
_____
_____
_____
_____
_____
_____
_____
_____
_____
_____
_____

- Cost (if any):

_____

✓ Keep everyone in the loop. Begin an Email/text list of potential and current clients.

TIP: Use sites good for email list management and mass texting.

- Site used (if any):

_____
_____

- Cost (if any):

_____

✓ Grab your cards, branding/marketing items and attend a few industry events locally to network.

TIP: Find and try a new one each month.

- Potential Networking Groups or Events to attend:

_____
_____
_____
_____
_____
_____
_____
_____
_____
_____
_____
_____
_____
_____
_____
_____
_____
_____

✓ Grab your cards, branding/marketing items and attend a few industry events OUTSIDE of your local comfort zone.

TIP: Find and try a new one each month.

- Potential Networking Groups or Events to attend:

_____
_____
_____
_____
_____

_____
_____
_____
_____
_____
_____
_____
_____
_____
_____

- ✓ Keep up with industry trends

    - ○ What are the current and coming trends in your industry:
_____
_____
_____
_____
_____
_____
_____
_____
_____
_____
_____
_____

- ✓ You can be a movement by yourself but a force when you're together! Connect and Collaborate with another or others.

TIP: Create an email and marketing packet to send out to businesses types listed

- ○ List types of businesses to collaborate with and how the connection works

ex. If a Fitness trainer collaborate with caterers who have healthy meal prep packages to grow client base.

_____
_____

_____
_____
_____
_____
_____
_____
_____
_____
_____
_____
_____
_____
_____
_____
_____
_____
_____
_____
_____
_____
_____
_____
_____
_____
_____
_____
_____
_____
_____
_____

- ✓ Go to Seminar specific for industry.
  - ○ Seminar:

_____
_____
_____

  - ○ Hosted by or Key Speaker:

_____
_____
_____

- Location:

_____
_____
_____

- Key Points Learned:

_____
_____
_____
_____
_____
_____
_____
_____
_____
_____
_____

- Cost (if any):

_____

✓ Learn everything you can. Take classes focused within industry for growth.

- Class type:

_____
_____

- Location of class:

_____
_____

- Date Started and Completed:

_____

- Key Points Learned:

_____
_____
_____
_____
_____
_____
_____
_____
_____
_____
_____
_____
_____
_____

- Cost (if any):

_____

✓ Read at least one entrepreneur or small business focused book a month

 - List potential books:

_____
_____
_____
_____
_____
_____
_____
_____
_____
_____
_____
_____
_____

_____
_____
_____

- ✓ Use information listed in your notebook to create a professional Business plan. Business plans can be simple or complex depending on what you need them for. Business plans to keep you personally on track can be simple. Business plans needed to present to other businesses can be a bit more detailed and complex. Google search templates to work for your current use.
    - o Date Completed:

_____
_____

KEEP GOING.

YOU GOT THIS!

➢ Bonus Business Task:

➤ **Bonus Business Task:**

> **Bonus Business Task:**

➢ NOTES:

➢ NOTES:

Thank you for your support.

Be sure to check out our other series in the 52 Week Experience.

www.the52weekexperience.com

Follow and share with us on IG @the52weekexperience

www.ingramcontent.com/pod-product-compliance
Lightning Source LLC
Chambersburg PA
CBHW071036080526
44587CB00015B/2645